LEADERSHIP

In Action

for Entrepreneurs

LYNNE ROE

Published October 2025

ISBN 979-8-9931598-1-2 paperback
ISBN 979-8-9931598-2-9 Hardcover
For information address:
The Three Tomatoes Book Publishing
6 Soundview Rd.
Glen Cove, NY 11542
www.thethreetomatoespublishing.com

Cover design: Tony Iatridis
Interior design: Tony Iatridis

the three
tomatoes
The Three Tomatoes Book Publishing

For the entrepreneurs who dare to dream, lead with courage, and make a meaningful impact—on their industries, their teams, and their communities.

CONTENTS

READER'S GUIDE
How to Use This Book

This book is designed to be simple and practical. Here's how to get the most out of it:

1. Read One Page a Week
- Start each week by reading one quote and commentary
- Reflect on how it applies to your business.

2. Take Action
- Put the suggested action into practice during the week.
- Small, consistent steps will create lasting habits.

3. Use the Three Tenets
- Each entry is labeled with one of the three leadership responsibilities:
  - Lead Your Business
  - Lead Your Team
  - Lead Yourself
- Focus on the area that matters most to you right now.

4. Turn to It When You Need It
- Facing a leadership challenge? Open the book to a page that speaks to your situation.
- Use it as a guide to help you take the next step forward.

Remember: this isn't a book to race through. It's a book to live with—week by week—as you grow into the leader your business and team need you to be.

INTRODUCTION

Running a business isn't easy. It takes vision, strategy, and the courage to lead. The truth is, your business won't grow just because you work harder. Long-term success comes when you step fully into your role as a leader.

But here's the question: are you leading your business to success—or are you letting circumstances lead your business?

To build a thriving company, every business owner must master three leadership responsibilities:

- Lead Your Business – Set the direction and create the systems that keep your business moving toward your goals.
- Lead Your Team – Build and develop a strong, capable team so you're not carrying the entire weight of the business on your shoulders.
- Lead Yourself – Grow into the kind of leader your business and team need—focused, resilient, and intentional.

This book is designed to help you strengthen each of these areas, one step at a time. On each page you'll find a quote about leadership followed by a short commentary on how to apply it in your business. I've also noted with each entry whether it ties to leading your business, leading your team, or leading yourself so you can easily connect the lesson to where you most need it.

To get the most out of this book, don't rush through it. It's not meant to be read cover-to-cover in one sitting. Instead, plan to read just one page a week. Choose the skill you want to work on, read the page, and consider taking the actions suggested. Or, when you're facing a leadership challenge, turn to the section that fits your situation and use it to focus on the next action that will move you forward. Small, consistent actions build strong habits—and strong habits build strong leaders.

As you move through these pages, know that you're not alone on this journey. I've written this book from my own experiences working with entrepreneurs who, like you, are committed to building something meaningful. My hope is that these weekly reflections give you clarity, courage, and encouragement to step fully into your role as a leader—and to create a business that truly supports the life you want.

~ *Lynne*

https:// leadershipinaction.net

To help you with your journey to lead your business, download these tools to help you put the book into action.

Get a simple worksheet to design a practical game plan, a quick self-assessment to reveal your strengths, and a 5-day micro-challenge to build momentum—so you can lead your business with clarity, confidence, and impact.

INNOVATION AND POSSIBILITIES

> ❝ Creativity is thinking up new things.
> Innovation is doing new things. ❞
>
> ~ *Theodore Levitt*

Innovation requires action!

What sets successful entrepreneurs apart is their willingness to act on those ideas quickly. Innovation isn't just about thinking differently—it's about doing something with those thoughts.

What idea have you been sitting on lately?

What is one action step you can take this week?

Lead Your Business

> Without change there is no innovation, creativity, or incentive for improvement. Those who initiate change will have a better opportunity to manage the change that is inevitable.
>
> ~ *William Pollard*

Lead the Change Before It Leads You!

Change can feel uncomfortable—but it's always coming. Great leaders don't wait for change to happen; they start it. When you take the lead, you have more influence over how things unfold and where they end up.

What's one change you'd like to see in your business right now?

Who do you need to connect with to initiate that change?

Lead Your Business

> " If you look at history, innovation doesn't come just from giving people incentives; it comes from creating environments where their ideas can connect. "
>
> ~ *Steven Johnson*

Innovation Grows in the Right Environment.

Much has been written about the importance of organizational culture. Great leaders understand that the environment they create can either inspire new ideas or shut them down.

This week, take a moment to look at your business.

How does your current environment support innovation—for you and your team?

Lead Your Team

> Listen to anyone with an original idea,
> no matter how absurd it may sound at first.
> If you put fences around people, you get
> sheep. Give people the room they need.
>
> ~ *William McKnight*

Listen First—Even to the Wild Ideas

The best ideas often come from the most unexpected places. That's why brainstorming works—even the wildest suggestion can spark something valuable.

As a leader, your role isn't to judge ideas too quickly. Instead, listen openly. Ask, "How could we make that work?" or "What else could help us reach that goal?"

By keeping the conversation going, you create trust. And even if an idea isn't possible right now, it may spark a truly great idea.

Lead Your Team

> ❝ You can have brilliant ideas, but
> if you can't get them across, your
> ideas won't get you anywhere. ❞
>
> ~*Lee Iacocca*

Ideas Only Matter When People Understand Them.

Great business leaders aren't just visionaries—they're clear communicators. They know how to connect their ideas to real goals and outcomes.

Before sharing a new idea, ask yourself: "What result are we trying to achieve?"

"How does this support our business objectives?"

Even bold, unusual ideas can succeed when they're tied to a clear purpose. So next time inspiration strikes, take a moment to ground it before sharing—it will help others see the value too.

Lead Yourself

> *It's not only moving that creates new starting points. Sometimes all it takes is a subtle shift in perspective, an opening of the mind, an intentional pause and reset, or a new route to start to see new options and new possibilities.*
>
> *~Kristin Armstrong*

A Fresh Perspective Can Open New Possibilities

As a business leader, you're always looking for what's possible.

Sometimes, all it takes is a fresh perspective to see new ideas and opportunities.

Talking with someone outside your usual circle — even from a different industry — can spark valuable insights you hadn't considered before.

This week, reach out to someone who sees things differently.

Have a conversation. You might just discover a new way forward.

Lead Your Business

> 66 Turn your obstacles into opportunities
> and your problems into possibilities. 99
>
> *~ Roy T. Bennett*

See the Possibility in Every Problem

Strong leaders don't get stuck when problems show up — they look for the opportunity inside the challenge.

When you face an obstacle this week, take a step back and ask:

"What new path could this open up for us?"

"What can we learn or do differently because of this?"

Lead Your Business

> Extraordinary people visualize not what is possible or probable, but rather what is impossible. And by visualizing the impossible, they begin to see it as possible.
>
> ~ *Cherie Carter-Scott*

Creative Thinking Can Lead To Fresh Solutions

Look at something that feels impossible and ask, "How could this be possible?"

That question opens the door for creative thinking and fresh solutions. You might not end up doing the impossible thing itself, but the process will often spark ideas that are both achievable and valuable for your business.

Try it this week with a few team members and see what possibilities you uncover.

Lead Your Team

> " I see possibilities in everything. For everything that's taken away, something of greater value has been given. "
>
> ~ *Michael J. Fox*

Look for the Possibilities in Change

When something is lost or taken away, it's easy to focus on what's missing.

But strong leaders train themselves to look for what might be gained instead.

Every change creates space for something new — a fresh idea, a better solution, or a different direction.

What's changed for you recently? What new possibilities could that change be making room for?

Lead Yourself

PASSION AND POSITIVITY

> " You have to be burning with an idea,
> or a problem, or a wrong that you want
> to right. If you're not passionate enough
> from the start, you'll never stick it out. "
>
> ~ *Steve Jobs*

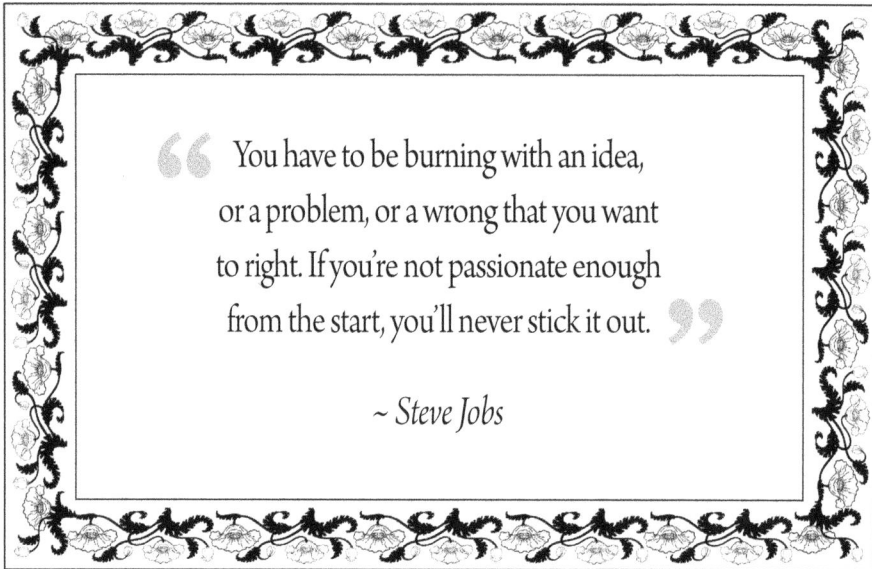

Let Passion Be Your Fuel

Your excitement and enthusiasm is contagious. When you're passionate about something, others feel it—and they're more likely to support your vision and help bring it to life.

Not every part of running a business is exciting. There are plenty of routine tasks. But strong leaders stay connected to the deeper impact of their work.

So ask yourself: What part of your work truly lights you up?

Hold onto that passion—it's what will keep you moving forward, even when things get tough.

Lead Yourself

> One person with passion is better
> than forty people merely interested.
>
> ~ E.M. Forster

Lead with Passion, and Others Will Follow

People are naturally drawn to leaders who are deeply committed to the impact they want to have on the world. When your team sees your passion, it inspires them to join you and give their best.

Let your energy and drive lead the way—and you'll build a team that's just as excited to create impact as you are.

Lead Your Team

> " My philosophy of leadership is to surround myself with good people who have ability, judgment and knowledge, but above all, a passion for service. "
>
> ~ *Sonny Perdue*

Great Leaders Serve First

Leadership is rooted in service, supporting and caring for others. As a leader, your job is to lift your team up, show them you care, and create an environment where they can thrive.

When you surround yourself with people who also have a heart for service, everyone grows—your team, your business, and the impact you make together.

How are you showing up to serve your team this week?

Lead Your Team

Leadership is the capacity to influence others through inspiration motivated by passion, generated by vision, produced by a conviction, ignited by a purpose.

~ Myles Munroe

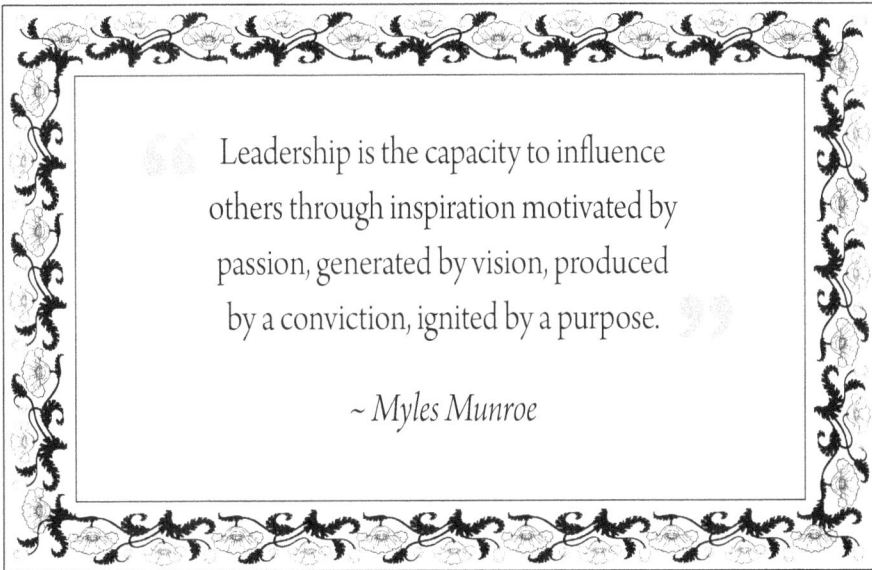

Lead Yourself with Purpose and Passion

Leaders inspire their team with combined passion, purpose, a clear vision and strong belief in their goals. That's the heart of true leadership.

Ask yourself: "Do I have all four—passion, purpose, vision, and conviction?"

If something's missing, what can you do this week to reignite your fire and lead with inspiration?

Lead Yourself

> " Positive leadership literally morphs
> the workplace from a place where people
> work at a job to one where they thrive. "
>
> ~Steve Gladis

Create a Workplace Where Your Team Thrives

Leaders set the mood for their team.

When the workplace feels positive, people are more motivated and do better work.

Consider this week how you can start each day with a positive attitude and bring that to your team. Try starting each day with a quick positive habit—like sharing a word of encouragement or celebrating a small win.

Lead Your Team

> " Great leadership usually starts
> with a willing heart, a positive attitude,
> and a desire to make a difference. "
>
> ~*Mac Anderson*

Lead with a Willing Heart and Positive Attitude

Great leaders show up with willingness, positivity, and a genuine desire to make a difference.

This week, try starting each day with something positive in mind.

Then ask yourself: How can I support each person on my team today?

Lead Yourself

> " Successful leaders see the opportunities
> in every difficulty rather than
> the difficulty in every opportunity. "
>
> ~ *Reed Markham*

See Opportunities in Every Challenge

We often get caught up in handling challenges when a different way of thinking could lead to a better result. Leaders are always looking for the opportunities.

This week, ask yourself: Where is the opportunity in the challenges we're facing?

And don't forget to ask your team—their perspective might surprise you.

Lead Yourself

> Each problem has hidden in it an opportunity so powerful that it literally dwarfs the problem. The greatest success stories were created by people who recognized a problem a turned it into an opportunity.
>
> ~ *Joseph Sugarman*

Look for the Hidden Opportunity

As a leader, your job is to spot opportunities where others only see problems—and then turn those opportunities into wins.

This week, take a fresh look at the challenges your business is facing. What possibilities are hiding inside them?

Lead Your Team

INFLUENCE AND CONNECTION

> 66 The key to successful leadership
> today is influence, not authority. 99
>
> ~ *Kenneth Blanchard*

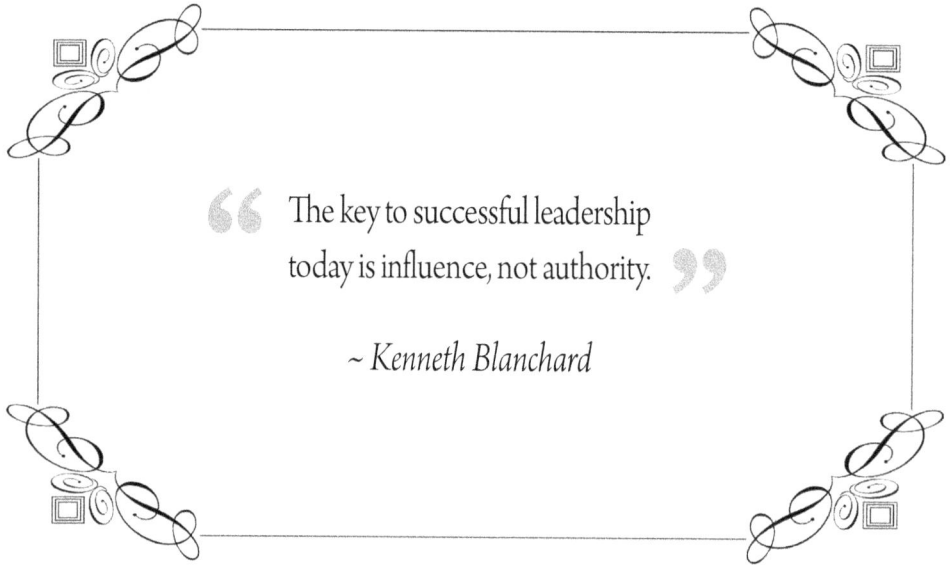

Leadership is About Influence and inspiring action

Influence means guiding how someone thinks or acts, not by force, but by connection and trust.

When entrepreneurs lead with influence instead of authority, their team chooses to follow them. And when people choose to follow, they're more committed and motivated in what they do.

How would a more committed team change your business?

And what's one thing you can do this week to build stronger trust and influence with your team?

Lead Your Team

> The length and breath of our influence
> on others are directly related to
> the depth of our concern for them.
>
> ~ John C. Maxwell

People Follow Leaders Who Truly Care

As a leader, your influence grows when people feel that you genuinely care about them.

This week, think about someone in your life or business who could use a little extra attention. Show up for them — whether that's through a conversation, support, or simply spending time together.

Then watch how your relationship begins to shift — not just this week, but in the months to come. Real leadership starts with real connection.

Lead Yourself

> " Leadership is not a matter of authority, it is a matter of influence. A true leader teaches others to understand more, motivates them to be more and inspires them to become more. "
>
> ~ *Michael Josephson*

Unlocking Potential Through Leadership

Great leaders don't just manage — they lift others up. They help their team grow, learn, and do more than they ever thought possible.

What's one thing you can do this week to support, encourage, or challenge your team?

How might your leadership unlock their potential?

Lead Your Team

> Leadership is the ability to influence people and motivate them to do what needs to be done to accomplish a goal, vision, or mission.
>
> ~*Robert Johnson*

Great Leaders Inspire a Shared Vision

Strong leaders always keep the bigger picture in mind — the goal, the vision, the mission.

But truly successful leaders go a step further: they bring their team along with them. They inspire, motivate, and create a shared sense of purpose.

This week, ask yourself: What can you do to help your team feel just as connected to your vision as you are? How can you invite them to take ownership and feel excited about reaching the goal together?

Lead Your Team

> ❝ You don't lead by pointing and telling people some place to go. You lead by going to that place and making a case. ❞
>
> *~Ken Kesey*

Lead by Living the Vision

Great leaders don't just talk about the destination — they envision the path first.

It starts with having a clear vision of the outcome you want. But to truly lead, you have to help your team see that vision too.

When people can picture the goal and believe in it, they're more likely to commit and give their best.

This week, think about this: What can you do to help your team not just hear your vision, but feel it — and want to make it real with you?

Lead Yourself

> The essence of leadership is relationship;
> influencing people to achieve things
> together that can't be achieved alone.
>
> ~*Leonard Sweet*

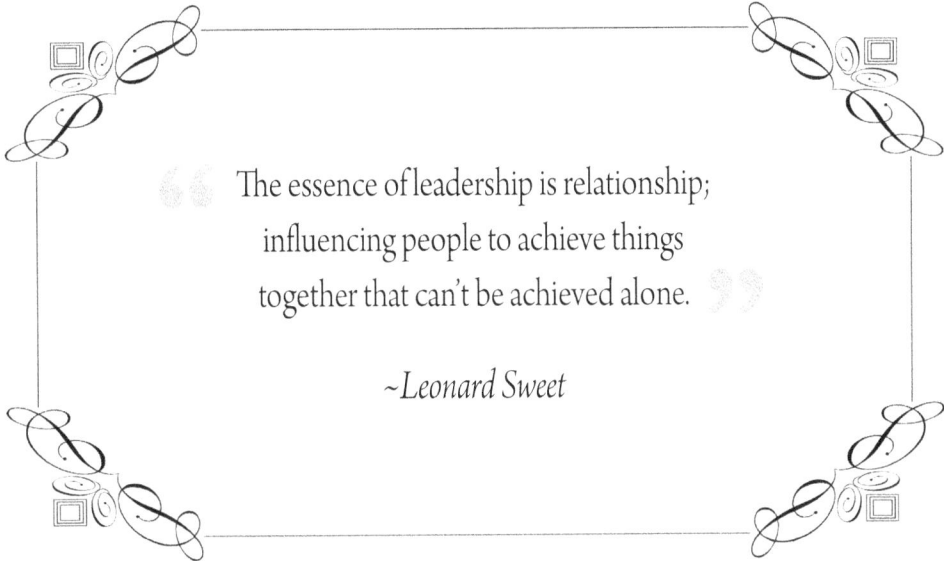

Stronger Together

Great leaders understand that real progress happens through relationships. When you bring people together, their unique perspectives help everyone see the bigger picture find the ideal solutions.

This week, take time to strengthen connections within your team. Encourage open conversations and welcome different points of view—you will build trust and create better solutions together.

Lead Your Team

> " A true leader has the ability to connect
> with their team, to understand
> their strengths, and to create a sense
> of purpose that motivates and inspires. "
>
> *~ Sheryl Sandberg*

Purpose-Driven Leadership Inspires Everyone

Whether your team is made up of full-time staff or part-time freelancers, your sense of purpose should guide and inspire them.

Strong leaders take time to learn what each person does best—and then connect those strengths to a shared goal. When everyone feels connected to the bigger purpose, they're more motivated to give their best.

Do your team members know how their contributions support the bigger picture?

Lead Your Team

> The best leaders are those who listen more than they talk, and are able to connect with their employees on a human level.
>
> *~ Richard Branson*

Great Leaders Listen Deeply

One of the most powerful qualities of a strong leader is the ability to focus and truly listen—not just to the words, but to the meaning behind them.

When you listen with full attention, you show others that you value them and what they have to say. It's one of the simplest and most meaningful ways to build trust and connection.

This week, take a moment to reflect: Are you really listening deeply in your conversations and building trust and connection?

Lead Yourself

> " Leadership is about building relationships, not just executing tasks. "
>
> ~ *John C. Maxwell*

Leadership Is About Connection, Not Just Completion

Being a leader isn't just about checking off tasks—it's about building strong, meaningful relationships.

This week, take a closer look at how you spend your time.

Are you focused more on getting things done or on connecting with the people around you to have the greatest impact with your work?

Small moments of connection can lead to big results.

Lead Your Business

PURPOSE AND INTENTIONAL

> 66 If leadership requires a fired-up sense of
> purpose and imagination, it also demands
> a profound connection to the society to be led. 99
>
> ~ *George Takei*

A Clear Purpose Inspires Others

Strong leaders have a clear purpose and a vision for the future. But real success comes when they share that vision in a way that excites and energizes others.

When you're clear about your purpose, it's easier to connect with people—and inspire them to join you.

This week, take a moment to reflect: Is your purpose clear? Who do you need to connect with to bring your vision to life?

Lead Your Team

> Leadership is the capacity to
> translate a vision into reality.
>
> ~ *Warren Bennis*

Turning vision into reality requires action

Having a vision is important—but true leadership means taking that vision and taking action.

It's not enough to dream. You have to act to make it a reality. What's one step you can take this week to bring your ideas to life?

Lead Your Business

> " Definiteness of purpose is the
> starting point of all achievement. "
>
> ~ *W. Clement Stone*

Clarity of Purpose Fuels Progress

Great leaders begin with a clear sense of purpose. It's what keeps them focused, motivated, and moving forward—even when things get tough.

This week, ask yourself: What area of your life or business needs a clearer purpose?

Take time to define it—because clarity is that starting point of success.

Lead Yourself

> To begin to think with purpose, is to enter the ranks of those strong ones who only recognize failure as one of the pathways to attainment.
>
> ~*James Allen*

Purpose Turns Failure into Fuel

Strong leaders stay focused on the outcome they're working toward. When things don't go as planned, they don't give up—they learn, adjust, and keep going.

Failure isn't the end. It's part of the path to success.

What can you learn from a recent setback that will help you move closer to your purpose?

Lead Yourself

> " *Intentional leadership means making conscious choices that lead to desired outcomes.* "
>
> ~*Chris Edmonds*

Intentional Leadership Starts With The Outcome In Mind

Strong leaders make decisions with a clear outcome in mind. They don't just react—they pause, consider their options, and then move forward with purpose. It's not about being slow—it's about being smart.

Think back: where have you acted without a clear outcome in mind?

What can you change in your decision making process to be more intentional this week?

Lead Your Business

> " Intentional leadership requires a clear vision, effective communication, and the ability to inspire others to action. "
>
> *~Richard Branson*

Lead with Vision, Inspire with Clarity

Great leaders begin with a clear vision—and then bring others along by helping them see it too.

Think about a project you're working on this week. Are you crystal clear on the outcome you're aiming for?

If not, take a moment to define it. The clearer you are, the easier it becomes to inspire and align your team.

What's one way you're bringing clarity and vision to your team this week?

Lead Your Team

> 66 Intentional leadership requires
> a commitment to ongoing
> learning and improvement. 99
>
> ~ *John F. Kennedy*

Lead Yourself First

Leaders are lifelong learners. They don't wait to grow by accident—they seek out the skills and knowledge that make them better at leading their team and business.

What's one thing you could learn or improve right now that would make you a stronger leader? What would be the impact of that change?

Take a moment to reflect—and then take action.

Lead Yourself

> *Intentional leaders understand that their legacy is not just about what they accomplish, but also about the impact they have on the lives of others.*
>
> *~ Maya Angelou*

Your Impact Multiplies When You Inspire and Uplift Others

A leader's true power is in their ability to influence and uplift others. That's how impact is multiplied—and how a legacy is built.

This week, ask yourself: Who can I inspire to support this vision?

And how can I help them move toward their own goals in the process?

Leadership isn't just about what you achieve—it's about who you help rise along the way.

Lead Yourself

43

> " *Intentional leadership is about having the courage to make difficult decisions and the compassion to listen to and understand others' perspectives.* "
>
> ~ *Brene Brown*

Decide with Courage, Lead with Compassion

Great leaders know how to make tough decisions—and they do it with heart.

They understand that every decision has consequences, not just for the business, but for the people involved.

It takes real courage to listen deeply to others' opinions, fears, and doubts—and still move forward with clarity.

Is there a difficult decision on your horizon?

Take the time to create space for honest conversations. Listen with compassion. Then lead with confidence.

Lead Your Team

CONTRIBUTION

> 66 True leadership lies in guiding others
> to success. In ensuring that everyone is
> performing at their best, doing the work
> they are pledged to do and doing it well. 99
>
> ~ *Bill Owens*

Support Your Team's Success

Strong leaders take responsibility for setting their team up to thrive.

That means making sure everyone has what they need—clear goals, the right tools, encouragement, space to grow and celebration for a job well done.

This week, ask yourself: "What does my team need most from me right now?"

Is it clarity? Resources? Motivation? Choose one area to focus on and take action.

When your team wins, so do you.

Lead Your Team

> It takes a lot of people to make
> a winning team. Everybody's
> contribution is important.
>
> *~ Gary David Goldberg*

Every Contribution Matters

Great leaders know that every team member plays a role in success.

They take time to recognize and appreciate those contributions—big or small.

Who on your team has made a difference this week?

Take a moment to say thank you. A little appreciation can go a long way.

Lead Your Team

> 66 Leadership is not about being in charge. Leadership is about taking care of those in your charge. 99
>
> ~ *Simon Sinek*

Lead by Supporting Others

Leadership isn't about being the boss—it's about caring for the people you lead.

Strong leaders focus on what their team needs to succeed. They pay attention to both the big picture and individual support, then step in to provide it.

Take a moment to reflect: How have you been showing up for your team?

What's one thing you can do this week to help them thrive?

Lead Yourself

> Serving people means growing their capacity and implies that everyone can contribute.
>
> ~*Juana Bordas*

Grow Your Team by Serving Them

Great leaders create a rich environment of support where their team can grow and succeed.

They know that everyone has something valuable to contribute—and that the leaders role is to support and nurture that potential.

Your team's success often depends on how well you serve them.

What's one way you can show up and support your team this week?

Lead Yourself

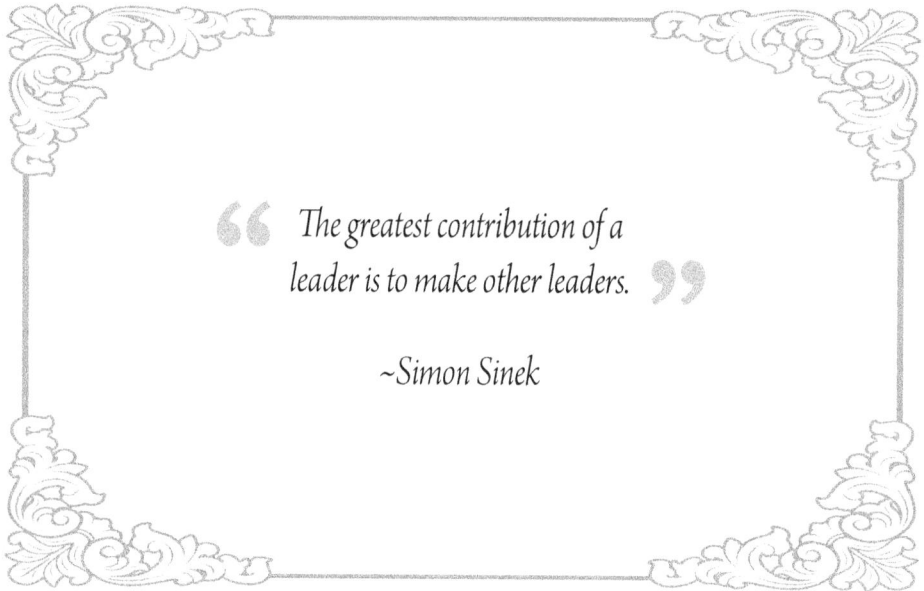

> 66 *The greatest contribution of a*
> *leader is to make other leaders.* 99
>
> ~*Simon Sinek*

Great leaders don't just lead—they build other leaders.

As an entrepreneur, one of the most powerful ways to grow your business is by helping others grow into leadership. When your team feels trusted and empowered, they rise to the challenge.

This week, ask yourself: "Who can I encourage to take more ownership? How can I create space for others to lead?"

Leadership is about impact—and that impact multiplies when you lift others up.

Lead Your Business

> Your job, as a leader, is to support
> your team with what they need to
> do their job to the best of their ability.
>
> *~Lynne Roe*

Leadership means serving first.

Your top job is to give your team the tools, guidance, and confidence they need to shine. When they succeed, the whole business moves forward.

This week, consider: Who could benefit from a quick check-in or extra resource? What small action can you take to clear a path for their success?

Support your team, and everyone—yourself included—will thrive.

Lead Your Team

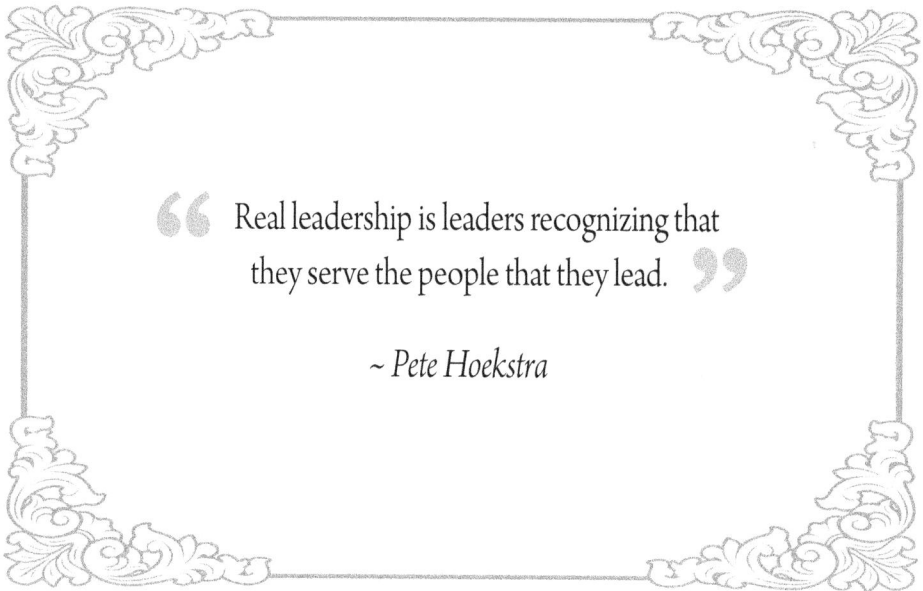

> " Real leadership is leaders recognizing that
> they serve the people that they lead. "
>
> ~ *Pete Hoekstra*

Leadership is service.

As an entrepreneur, your role isn't just to direct—it's to support. Real leadership means showing up in ways that help your team do their best work.

This week, take a moment to reflect: Are my actions helping my team grow and succeed? What's one thing I can adjust to better support them?

Small shifts in how you lead can make a big difference in how your team thrives.

Lead Yourself

> *Leadership is ultimately about creating*
> *a way for people to contribute to*
> *making something extraordinary happen.*
>
> ~ Alan Keith

Extraordinary things happen when people feel the work they do matters.

When your team feels they're part of something meaningful, they show up with energy, purpose, and their best work.

As a leader, it's your job to bring focus, direction, and thoughtful planning—so everyone knows how their skills make a difference.

This week, ask yourself: "What's one thing I can do to help my team contribute more confidently? How can I create space for them to do their best work?"

Great results start with great leadership.

Lead Your Business

> *I think leadership is service and there is power in that giving: to help people, to inspire and motivate them to reach their fullest potential.*
>
> ~ Denise Morrison

Leadership is about lifting others up.

When you support and encourage your team to grow into their best selves, everyone benefits. Each person thrives—and your entire business becomes stronger.

This week, think about how you can inspire your team to stretch, grow, and succeed.

Great leaders bring out the greatness in others.

Lead Your Team

LEARNING AND GROWTH

> 66 Leadership and learning are
> indispensable to each other. 99
>
> ~ *John F. Kennedy*

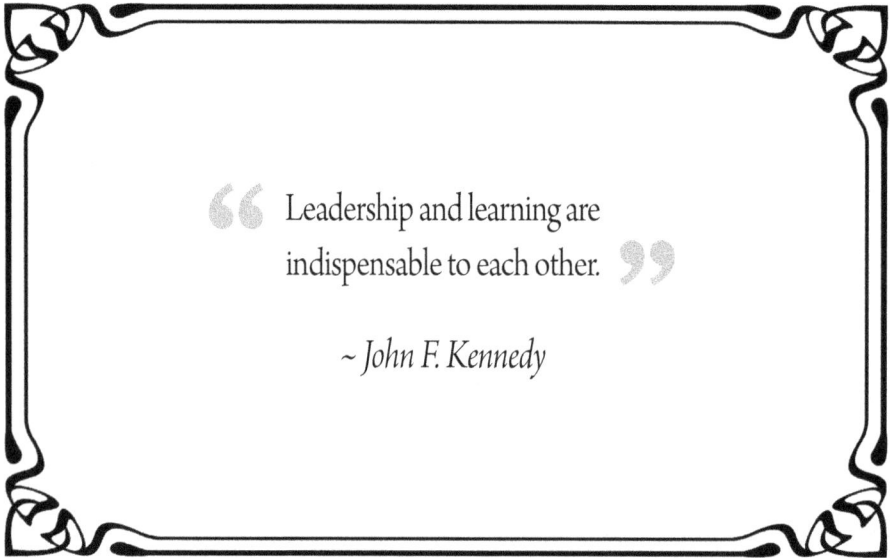

Great Leaders Never Stop Learning

Smart leaders know that learning isn't optional—it's essential for growth and long-term success. And it's not just for them—every level of the business benefits when learning becomes part of the culture.

This week, challenge yourself and your team with questions like: "What can we learn from this experience?" or "Who can offer insight to help us improve our service or product?"

Regularly asking questions like these will help you quickly improve everything you do.

Lead Your Business

> Learning is not a one-time event
> or a periodic luxury. Great leaders
> in great companies recognize that the
> ability to constantly learn, innovate,
> and improve is vital to their success.
>
> ~ *Amy Edmondson*

Learning Is a Leadership Habit

Strong leaders make learning a regular part of their routine—not just something they do once in a while. They ask, "What do I need to learn next?" and then take action.

This week, take a moment to reflect: What are you learning right now that will help you grow as a leader or improve your business?

Lead Yourself

> " A true leader never stops being a student, always learning, improving. "
>
> ~ *Lakeisha M Williams*

Curious Leaders Stay Ready

Great leaders are lifelong students. Their curiosity drives them to keep learning, growing, and staying prepared for whatever comes next.

And when leaders model curiosity, it inspires their whole team to grow, too.

This week, ask yourself: What are you curious about right now? What's one thing you want to learn?

Lead Yourself

> The ability to learn is the most
> important quality a leader can have.
>
> *~Sheryl Sandberg*

Great Leaders Are Fast Learners

Leaders often face new challenges—things they've never done before. The ability to learn quickly and make smart decisions is one of the most valuable skills a leader can have.

This week, reflect on this: What's your process for learning something new—fast?

Sharpen that skill, and you'll lead your team with more confidence and clarity.

Lead Your Team

> " *Unless you try to do something beyond what you have already mastered, you will never grow.* "
>
> ~*Ralph Waldo Emerson*

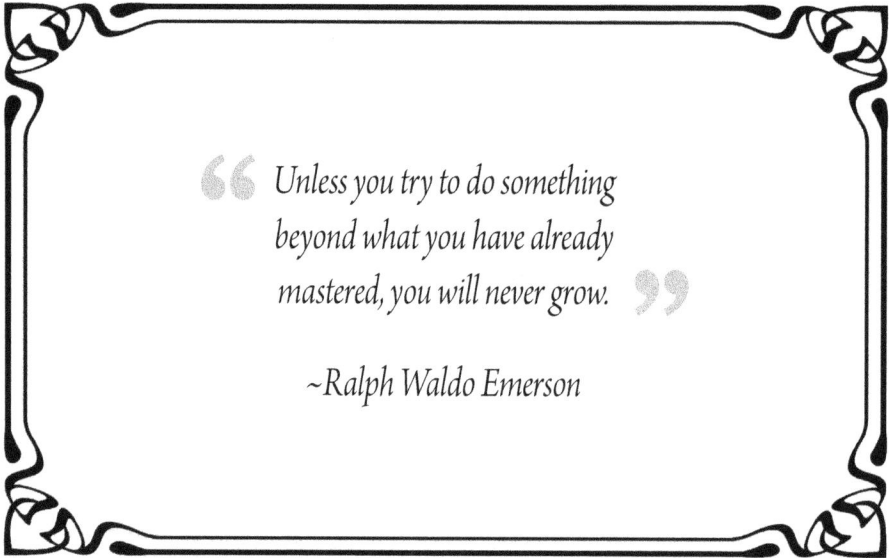

Growth Happens With Continuous Learning

Great leaders never stop learning. Even when they've mastered a skill, they don't settle — they keep pushing to grow, improve, and reach the next level.

This week, think about a skill you've already mastered. What could you do to take it even further?

Growth doesn't come from standing still — it comes from stretching just beyond what you already know.

Lead Yourself

> *Before you are a leader, success is all about growing yourself. When you become a leader, success is all about growing others.*
>
> ~Jack Welch

A Leader's Success Comes from Helping Others Succeed

Your role isn't just to lead — it's to support, guide, and empower each team member to do their best work.

This week, take a moment to ask yourself: "What does each person on my team need to succeed? And how can I help provide that support?"

Lead Your Team

> 66 Continuous improvement is
> better than delayed perfection. 99
>
> ~ *Mark Twain*

Small Improvements Lead to Big Results

As a small business leader, you know that big changes rarely happen overnight.

But success comes from steady, continuous improvement — even just 1% improvement compounds over time.

Great leaders are always asking, how can we make this better?

This week, take a fresh look at your business.

What's one area you could improve by just 1%?

Lead Your Business

> *A good objective of leadership is to help those who are doing poorly to do well and to help those who are doing well to do even better.*
>
> ~ Jim Rohn

Great Leaders Help Everyone Grow

Strong leaders know that everyone — no matter where they're starting from — has room to grow.

They take time to understand each team member and give them the support they need to do even better.

Because growth doesn't look the same for everyone.

This week, ask yourself: "What does each person on my team need right now to thrive?

And how can I help them take their next step forward?"

Lead Your Team

ACTION AND COMMITMENT

> " Success seems to be connected with
> action. Successful people keep moving.
> They make mistakes, but they don't quit. "
>
> ~ *Conrad Hilton*

Keep Moving, Even When It's Messy

No leader or business gets it right every time. But successful leaders don't let mistakes stop them—they adjust their approach and keep moving toward their goal.

This week, ask yourself: "Where can we shift our strategy—not our goal—to keep making progress?"

Lead Yourself

None of it works unless YOU work.
We have to do our part. If
knowing is half the battle, action
is the second half of the battle.

~ Jim Kwik

Knowing Isn't Enough—You Have to Act

Many of us already know what we need to do to succeed—but only those who take action actually move forward.

The key to a leader's success is doing, not just knowing.

This week, ask yourself: "What's one thing we've been putting off?"

Take a small step toward it today. Once you start, momentum will follow.

Lead Yourself

> " When you do the things in the present that you can
> see, you are shaping the future that you are yet to see. "
>
> *~Idowu Koyenikan*

Lead Today. Shape Tomorrow.

Great leaders always keep the future in mind. By sharing a clear and inspiring vision, you help your team take meaningful action today—action that shapes the future you're all working toward.

This week, ask yourself: What's one thing you can say or do to inspire your team to take action now?

Lead Your Team

> " Patience, more than the ability to bear pains
> or endure waiting, is to be calm no matter
> what happens – constantly take action to
> turn it to positive growth opportunities
> – and have faith to believe that it will all
> work out in the end while you are waiting. "
>
> *~Roy T. Bennett*

Patience in Business Means Progress with Purpose

Change doesn't happen overnight—and great leaders know that.

They stay focused on the outcome, keep taking small, consistent steps forward, and learn from the setbacks along the way.

Success comes from patience, persistence, and the belief that progress—no matter how slow—still counts.

This week, remind yourself to: Stay calm, learn, and keep moving forward.

Lead Your Business

> ❝ *Commitment is the enemy of resistance, for it is the serious promise to press on, to get up, no matter how many times you are knocked down.* ❞
>
> *~David McNally*

Commitment Keeps You Moving Forward

Challenges are part of the journey. We all face setbacks, delays, and moments that knock us off course.

But great leaders don't give up — they stay committed.

It's that commitment that keeps them going, even when things get tough.

How strong is your commitment right now? What goal do you need to recommit to in order to keep moving forward?

Lead Yourself

> *Desire is the key to motivation, but it's determination and commitment to an unrelenting pursuit of your goal - a commitment to excellence - that will enable you to attain the success you seek.*
>
> *~Mario Andretti*

Is "Good Enough" Holding You Back?

Wanting success is a great start — but it's not enough.

To truly reach your goals, you need determination and a strong commitment to doing your best work. Sometimes, "good enough" just isn't enough.

Which of your business goals would benefit from raising the bar?

This week, take a closer look: Where can you commit to excellence — and not just getting by?

Lead Your Business

71

> " *The kind of commitment I find among the best performers across virtually every field is a single-minded passion for what they do, an unwavering desire for excellence in the way they think and the way they work.* "
>
> ~ Jim Collins

Are You Truly Committed to Excellence?

Great leaders exhibit a relentless dedication to their craft and a singular passion for their work. They pursue excellence with unwavering determination, consistently seeking improvement in all areas.

This week, ask yourself: "How committed am I to excellence — in the way I think, work, and lead? What's one area where I can raise the standard?"

Lead Yourself

> *You're not obligated to win. You're obligated to keep trying to do the best you can every day.*
>
> ~ Marian Wright Edelman

Focus on Progress, Not Perfection

As leaders, our primary duty isn't solely about achieving our goals at all costs, but rather about consistently striving for excellence. Each day presents an opportunity to push ourselves to perform to the best of our abilities, regardless of the outcome.

This week, take a look at one area of your life or business that could benefit from steady progress. What might be possible if you simply committed to getting a little better each day?

Lead Yourself

> *Individual commitment to a group effort - that is what makes a team work, a company work, a society work, a civilization work.*
>
> *~ Vince Lombardi*

Commitment Is What Makes Teams Work

As a leader, one of your most important jobs is to help each person on your team see how their effort matters. When everyone shows up fully and contributes with commitment, real progress happens — whether it's in a business, a project, or a community.

This week, take a moment to ask yourself: "What can I do to inspire greater commitment in my team?" A small shift in energy from each person can lead to big results.

Lead Your Team

PLANNING AND PREPARATION

> " Setting a goal is not the main thing. It is deciding how you will go about achieving it and staying with that plan. "
>
> ~ *Tom Landry*

Goals Are Just the Beginning

Setting a goal can spark excitement and give you direction — but that alone won't get you across the finish line.

Leaders know it is the actions you take every day toward that goal that matter most. Staying consistent and focused is what turns a goal into a result.

This week, as you think about your future goals, take it one step further:

What specific actions will you commit to — and stick with — to make those goals happen?

Lead Yourself

> Every minute you spend in planning saves
> 10 minutes in execution; this gives you
> a 1,000 percent return on energy!
>
> ~ *Brian Tracy*

Smart Planning Saves Time and Energy

Planning isn't just about being organized — it's about staying ahead.

Strong leaders take time to think through possible roadblocks before they happen. That way, they can avoid setbacks and keep things moving forward smoothly.

This week, look at what you're working on. What could possibly get in the way of your success? What simple steps can you take now to prevent those challenges later?

Lead Your Business

> *Planning is bringing the future into the present so that you can do something about it now.*
>
> ~Alan Lakein

Bring the Future Into the Present

Great leaders look ahead, spot challenges and opportunities, and take action now to shape the future they want.

They bring their team into the planning process—sharing the vision, inspiring buy-in, and working together to map out the path forward.

When the whole team helps build the plan, they're more committed to making it happen.

Lead Your Team

> *A goal without a plan is just a wish.*
>
> *~Antoine de Saint-Exupéry*

Create a Plan to Make Goals Happen

Great leaders don't just set goals—they create a plan to make them happen.

A solid plan helps you spot potential challenges, prepare for them, and stay on track until you reach your goal.

Have you set a goal without a clear plan? This week, take the time to map out the steps that will get you there.

Lead Yourself

> *There are no secrets to success. It is the result of preparation, hard work, and learning from failure.*
>
> *~Colin Powell*

Success Starts with Preparation

It's tempting to say, "We've done this before — let's just take action." But jumping in without proper preparation can lead to avoidable mistakes.

Smart leaders take the time to plan ahead. Preparation helps you spot potential issues early and put solutions in place before they become problems.

This week, ask yourself: "Where could a little extra preparation lead to a better outcome?"

Lead Your Business

> " *Good luck is when opportunity meets preparation, while bad luck is when lack of preparation meets reality.* "
>
> *~Eliyahu Goldratt*

Preparation Turns Opportunity into Success

When you and your team are prepared, you can act quickly and take advantage of opportunities as they come.

But when you're not ready, those same opportunities can slip away — simply because you weren't in a position to act.

This week, take a moment to ask: "What can I and my team do now to be ready when the next opportunity shows up?"

Lead Your Team

> *I believe that people make their own luck*
> *by great preparation and good strategy.*
>
> *~ Jack Canfield*

Luck Favors the Prepared

It's easy to look at successful people and think they just got lucky. More often than not, their "luck" came from planning ahead and being ready when the right opportunity came along.

They thought about what could happen — and built a strategy to meet it when it did.

This week, ask yourself: What opportunities are out there for you and your team?

And what can you do now to be ready when they arrive?

Lead Your Team

> *One important key to success is self-confidence.*
> *An important key to self-confidence is preparation.*
>
> *~ Arthur Ashe*

Preparation Builds Confidence — and Success

When you take time to prepare, you feel more capable, more focused, and more ready to handle challenges as they come.

That preparation builds self-confidence — because you know you've done the work. And every small win along the way makes you even more confident for the next step.

This week, ask yourself: What can you do to prepare — so you and your team are ready to succeed?

Lead Yourself

> *Proper preparation prevents poor performance.*
>
> *~ James Baker*

Preparation Leads to Confidence and Success

Most people fear poor performance — but great leaders know how to face that fear: with preparation.

When you take time to prepare, you boost your chances of success and feel more confident going in.

This week, carve out time in your calendar to prepare for an upcoming challenge.

A little preparation now can make a big difference later.

Lead Yourself

ASSERTIVENESS AND OUT OF YOUR COMFORT ZONE

> ❝ *To be passive is to let others decide for you. To be aggressive is to decide for others. To be assertive is to decide for yourself. And to trust that there is enough, that you are enough.* ❞
>
> ~ *Edith Eva Eger*

Assertive Leadership Starts with Respect

Great leaders know how to speak their truth without stepping on others. They aren't passive — staying silent when something matters — and they aren't aggressive — making decisions for others.

Instead, they're assertive. They communicate clearly, stand their ground, and still respect different opinions.

This week, reflect on your recent interactions: Were there times you stayed quiet when you should have spoken up? Or times you pushed too hard instead of listening?

Notice where you can lead with more balance — by trusting yourself and creating space for others.

Lead Yourself

> *Being assertive does not mean attacking or ignoring others feelings. It means that you are willing to hold up for yourself fairly - without attacking others.*
>
> ~ Albert Ellis

Assertive Leadership Starts with Respect

Strong leaders respect the thoughts and feelings of others, as well as their own thoughts and feelings.

They know how to speak up honestly while still listening with care. It's not about staying quiet or being forceful — it's about finding the balance that comes from mutual respect.

This week, ask yourself: "How can I express myself more clearly while still honoring others?"

What small shift can you make to lead with both confidence and kindness?

Lead Yourself

> " Assertiveness is not what you do, it's who you are! "
>
> ~ *Shakti Gawain*

Assertiveness Shows Up in How You Lead

Assertiveness isn't just about what you say — it's how you show up every day.

Strong leaders lead with clarity, confidence, and respect. They honor their own values and the voices of their team.

As you lead your business, take a moment to reflect:

Are your actions showing respect for both yourself and your team?

Lead Your Team

> *The basic difference between being assertive and being aggressive is how our words and behavior affect the rights and well-being of others.*
>
> *~Sharon Anthony Bower*

Great Leaders Set the Tone

As a leader, you're not only responsible for your own actions — you also shape how your team interacts with one another.

This week, take a closer look:

Are your team members showing respect for each other's rights, ideas, and well-being?

Remember, your example sets the tone. The way you lead creates the culture around you.

Lead Your Team

> " *Step out of your comfort zone. Comfort zones,*
> *where your unrealized dreams are buried,*
> *are the enemies of achievement. Leadership*
> *begins when you step outside your comfort zone.* "
>
> *~Roy T. Bennett*

Growth Lives Outside Your Comfort Zone

Real growth doesn't happen by doing what you've always done. It begins when you step into something new — something a little uncomfortable.

As the leader of your business, ask yourself: "Where do I need to stretch to reach the next level?"

This week, choose one area where you know growth is needed — and make a plan to take that next bold step.

Lead Your Business

> *Coming out of your comfort zone is tough in the beginning, chaotic in the middle, and awesome in the end. . . because in the end, it shows you a whole new world !! Make an attempt.*
>
> ~*Manoj Arora*

Leaders know that starting something new is never easy.

Stretching beyond your comfort zone can feel uncomfortable and messy at first. But this discomfort is part of growing and changing.

Keep your thoughts on the outcome you want, and remember—pushing through the rough spots opens the door to something great.

This week, what's one small step you can take outside your comfort zone? Commit to taking it, and notice what you learn.

Lead Yourself

> ❝ *The comfort zone is the great enemy to creativity;*
> *moving beyond it necessitates intuition, which in turn*
> *configures new perspectives and conquers fears.* ❞
>
> ~*Dan Stevens*

Leaders know that staying in the comfort zone limits creativity and progress.

Leaders work with their team to see things in new ways, face fears, and take action.

Ask yourself: Where is your team stuck in their comfort zone?

What fresh perspective can you share to help them move forward?

This week, pick one way to challenge your team's thinking and encourage them to take a step beyond what feels comfortable.

Lead Your Team

> *Move out of your comfort zone. You can only grow if you are willing to feel awkward and uncomfortable when you try something new.*
>
> ~ *Brian Tracy*

Taking the next step means being brave.

If you're like most leaders, you got where you are by trying new things and stepping outside your comfort zone.

Taking the next step usually means being brave enough to face some discomfort and try something different.

What's your next move? Where do you need to find the courage to try something new?

Lead Yourself

CONSISTENCY AND MOMENTUM

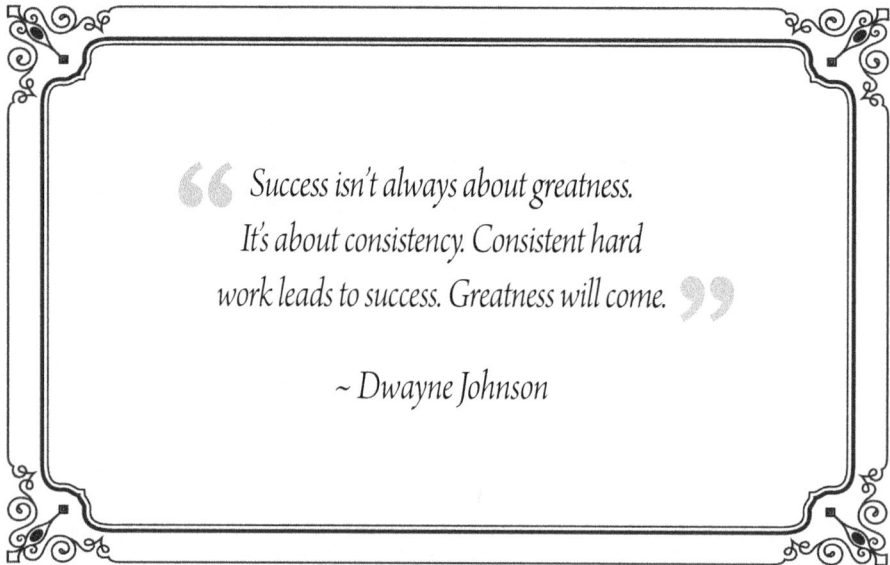

> 66 *Success isn't always about greatness.*
> *It's about consistency. Consistent hard*
> *work leads to success. Greatness will come.* 99
>
> ~ *Dwayne Johnson*

Great leaders succeed with consistent hard work

This week, take a moment to reflect on what you do consistently that helps you move forward.

Successful entrepreneurs know that it's not just about big wins — it's about showing up every day and doing the small things that add up over time. Great leaders often have simple routines, both in their personal life and business, that keep them on track.

What routines do you rely on? Is there one small action you could add to an existing routine — or one new habit you've been meaning to start?

Lead Yourself

> *Small disciplines repeated with*
> *consistency every day lead to great*
> *achievements gained slowly over time.*
>
> *~ John C. Maxwell*

What small habits are helping you move toward your goals?

Strong leaders understand that while some goals require a big push, many are achieved through steady, consistent effort over time.

Think about your daily routines. What small action have you already built into your day that keeps you on track? And what's one simple habit you could add this week — something small you can do every day — that will pay off in the long run?

Success doesn't always happen in big leaps. Often, it's the quiet, repeated steps that get you there.

Lead Yourself

> ❝ *Successful people do ordinary things with extraordinary consistency, commitment and focus.* ❞
>
> ~*Jon Gordon*

This week, take a closer look at the everyday things you and your team do.

How consistent are you with them? Often, it's the simple, ordinary tasks — done with steady focus — that lead to big results.

Pick one or two of those small actions that could make a real difference if done more consistently. Make a plan. Stick to it.

Then pay attention to the impact of your consistent actions.

Lead Your Team

> *Success doesn't come from what you do occasionally, it comes from what you do consistently.*
>
> ~Marie Forlio

Where could more consistency make a difference in your business?

This week, take a step back and look at the areas in your business that would improve with steady, repeated action.

Now ask yourself — can any of these be streamlined or automated to make consistency easier?

A small system or routine put in place today can lead to big results over time.

Lead Your Business

> 66 *The most important thing you can do to achieve*
> *your goals is to make sure that as soon as you set*
> *them you immediately begin to create momentum.* 99
>
> ~Tony Robbins

Set your goal and take action

When you set a goal, the key to success is building momentum right away. Take an immediate step—no matter how small—to get started. Momentum begins with action, but commitment keeps it going. Stay committed by taking consistent, intentional steps forward.

What action will you take today to build momentum?

Lead Yourself

> *One overlooked ingredient to successful organizations and leaders is the ability to create and sustain momentum.*
>
> *~Ken Gosnell*

Great leaders build and sustain momentum

Once you set a goal, identify the key actions that will move you forward—and take them consistently. But momentum isn't just about starting strong; it's about keeping the pace.

Think of your business like a bicycle—it won't move on its own. You have to keep pedaling, even with small pushes, to stay in motion.

What's your next push to keep the momentum going?

Lead Your Business

> " *The engine of your business isn't you, your product, nor your stellar supply chain—it's the momentum you have. The only true job of a leader is to inspire momentum in their teams and then ensure this movement is heading in the right direction.* "
>
> ~ *Raj Jana*

Your role as a leader is to fuel team momentum

How can you keep your team inspired, especially when tasks feel repetitive? Do they see the value in their work? Do they understand how it connects to the bigger picture?

A motivated team moves faster and further. Find ways to make the process engaging—maybe even fun!

How will you energize your team today?

Lead Your Team

> *The rhythm of daily action aligned with your goals creates the momentum that separates dreamers from super-achievers.*
>
> ~ Darren Hardy

Momentum comes from consistent action.

Great leaders don't wait for progress to happen—they create it. They choose their actions deliberately and commit to them daily.

What actions have you committed to that will move you and your business forward?

Lead Yourself

CREATIVITY AND IMAGINATION

> *The role of a creative leader is not to have all the ideas; it's to create a culture where everyone can have ideas and feel that they're valued.*
>
> ~ Ken Robinson

Fostering creativity and innovation within the team is a critical role for a leader.

When your team feels safe to share and explore new ways of doing things, creativity and innovation naturally follow.

This week, take time to brainstorm with your team. Pick one thing you're currently doing and explore how it could be done better or more efficiently.

Welcome every idea — even the ones that seem impossible. Sometimes, those impossible ideas spark the best solutions that are possible.

Lead Your Team

> *Creativity is not just for artists. It's for businesspeople looking for a new way to close a sale; it's for engineers trying to solve a problem; it's for parents who want their children to see the world in more than one way.*
>
> ~ Twyla Tharp

Creativity isn't just for artists — it's a powerful tool for business success.

Encouraging creative ideas and solutions is a critical skill for a business leader. Often, the best solutions come when you step outside the usual way of thinking.

What current challenge in your business could use a fresh approach?

Try looking at it from a different angle:

- Imagine the problem is already solved — what steps might have led you there?
- Look at it through someone else's eyes — a client, team member, or partner.
- Or gather your team and brainstorm freely, with no judgment.
- Let your imagination lead.

Lead Your Business

> ❝ *The entrepreneur always searches for change, responds to it and exploits it as an opportunity.* ❞
>
> *~Peter Drucker*

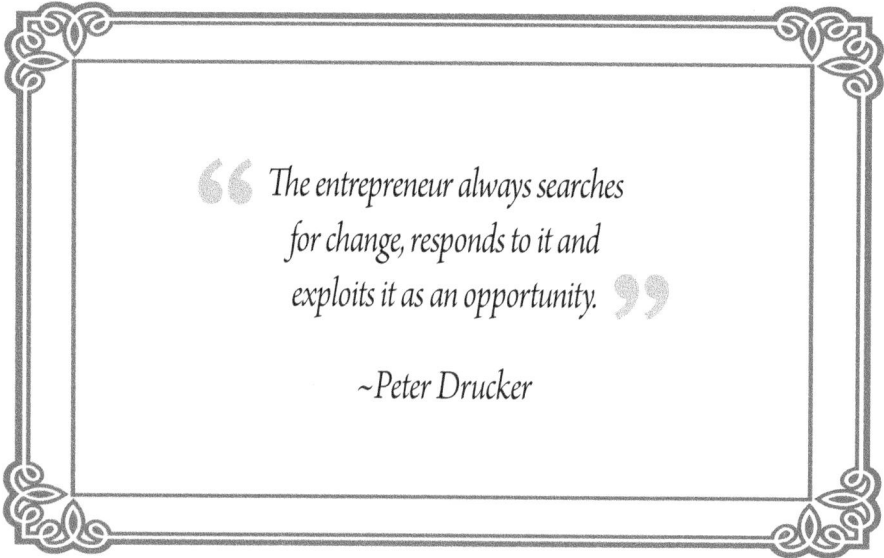

Great entrepreneurs don't just adapt to change — they turn it into opportunity.

As a business leader, learning to see change as a chance to grow is a valuable skill. It takes creativity and a willingness to think differently.

This week, look at a current challenge or change in your business with fresh eyes.

What new opportunity could it be offering you?

How can you respond in a way that moves your business forward?

Lead Your Business

> *Creativity is intelligence having fun.*
>
> ~*Albert Einstein*

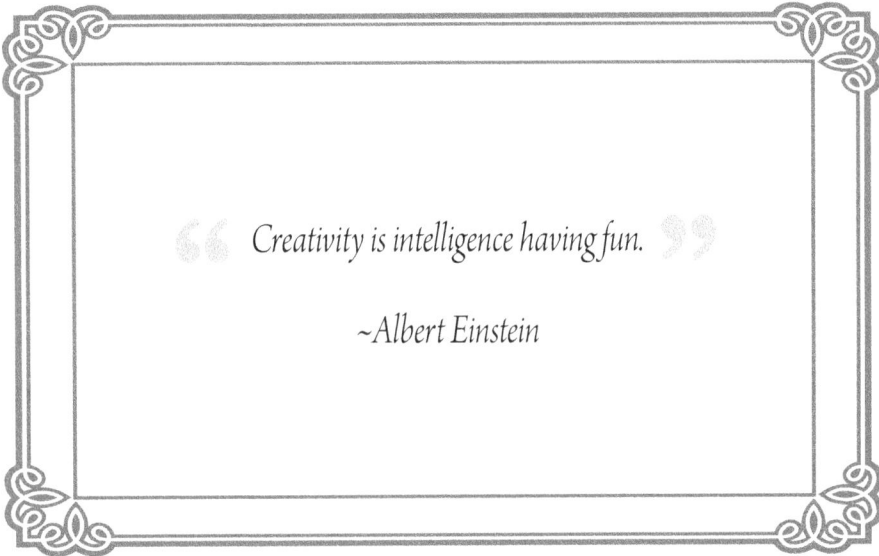

Bringing fun into the business brings fresh ideas.

Smart teams often stay laser-focused on goals — which is great, but sometimes too much focus can limit creative thinking.

When you bring a little fun into the process, it opens the door for fresh ideas and new ways of solving problems.

This week, look for simple ways to lighten the mood during team meetings. A quick game, a fun question, or a relaxed brainstorming session can help your team think more creatively — and enjoy the process, too.

Lead Your Team

> *I apply the term 'creativity' broadly...*
> *it's problem-solving. We are all faced*
> *with problems, and we have to address*
> *them and think of something new,*
> *and that's where creativity comes in.*
>
> *~Edwin Catmull*

Creativity is problem-solving.

Running a business means solving problems — over and over again. And since no two situations are exactly the same, each one calls for fresh thinking.

Creative problem-solving isn't just a skill — it's a mindset that helps your business grow and adapt.

What's one challenge you're facing right now that could benefit from a fresh approach?

Lead Your Business

> *Our intuition and imagination lead
> us to fresh thinking with which
> we can creatively manage change.*
>
> ~Linda Naiman

Change is a constant challenge for leaders

The best leaders use their imagination to create a clear vision of where they're headed—and they make sure their team sees it too. How clear are you on what you're building? Take some time this week to imagine the outcome you want, then share that vision with your team. When everyone is aligned, change becomes much easier to manage.

Lead Your Team

> *All successful people men and women are big dreamers. They imagine what their future could be, ideal in every respect, and then they work every day toward their distant vision, that goal or purpose.*
>
> ~ Brian Tracy

Imagine the future you want

Great leaders take time to imagine the future they want.

Once they have a clear vision, they take consistent steps to make it a reality.

This week, take a moment to picture the future you're working toward. What's one action you can take today to bring that vision closer?

Lead Yourself

> *The very essence of leadership is that you have to have vision. You can't blow an uncertain trumpet.*
>
> ~ *Theodore M. Hesburgh*

What can your business become?

Great leaders don't just see their business as it is—they imagine what it can become. A strong leader has a clear vision of the future and moves toward it with confidence. You don't need to have all the answers on how to get there—that's where your team comes in. Your job is to define the destination and lead with conviction.

Lead Your Business

> " *A leader's job is to look into the future and see the organization, not as it is, but as it should be.* "
>
> ~ Jack Welch

Think about your business as it should be

What does the future of your business look like—not as it is now, but as it should be? Take some time this week to envision that future, then take one step to bring it closer to reality.

Lead Your Business

> *Reason can answer questions,*
> *but imagination has to ask them.*
>
> ~ *Ralph Gerard*

What questions should you be asking?

Great leaders don't just look for answers—they ask the right questions. Questions like, "What could we do differently?" "What is the long-term potential of this business?" or "What haven't we considered yet?"

This week, take a moment to reflect. What important questions haven't you asked yourself yet?

Lead Yourself

LISTENING AND EMOTIONAL INTELLIGENCE

> *It is the province of knowledge to speak.*
> *And it is the privilege of wisdom to listen.*
>
> ~ Oliver Wendell Holmes

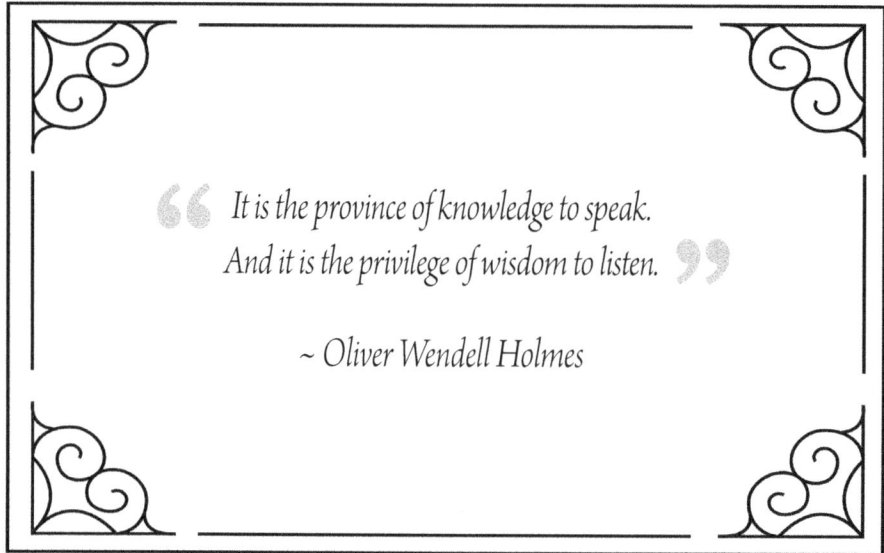

Wise leaders listen.

Listening is one of the most powerful — and often overlooked — skills a leader can develop.

Strong leaders don't just hear words; they pay close attention to what's being said by clients, colleagues, team members, friends, and family. Instead of jumping to respond or filtering things through their own assumptions, they pause, reflect, and seek to understand.

Then they acknowledge or clarify what was said — letting the other person know they were truly heard and valued.

This week, pay attention to how you're listening. Are you filtering, or are you fully considering what was said?

Lead Yourself

> *To say that a person feels listened to means a lot more than just their ideas get heard. It's a sign of respect. It makes people feel valued.*
>
> ~ Deborah Tannen

Listening is a powerful way to show respect.

Great leaders earn trust by giving their full attention when someone speaks. When you truly listen — without distractions, interruptions, or rushing to respond — you're showing that you care.

It tells your team their thoughts and ideas matter. And that simple act can make a big difference.

This week, ask yourself: Who needs your full attention today? How can you show them they're truly heard and valued?

Lead Your Team

> *Of all the skills of leadership, listening is the most valuable — and one of the least understood. Most captains of industry listen only sometimes, and they remain ordinary leaders. But a few, the great ones, never stop listening. That's how they get word, before anyone else, of unseen problems and opportunities.*
>
> ~Peter Nulty

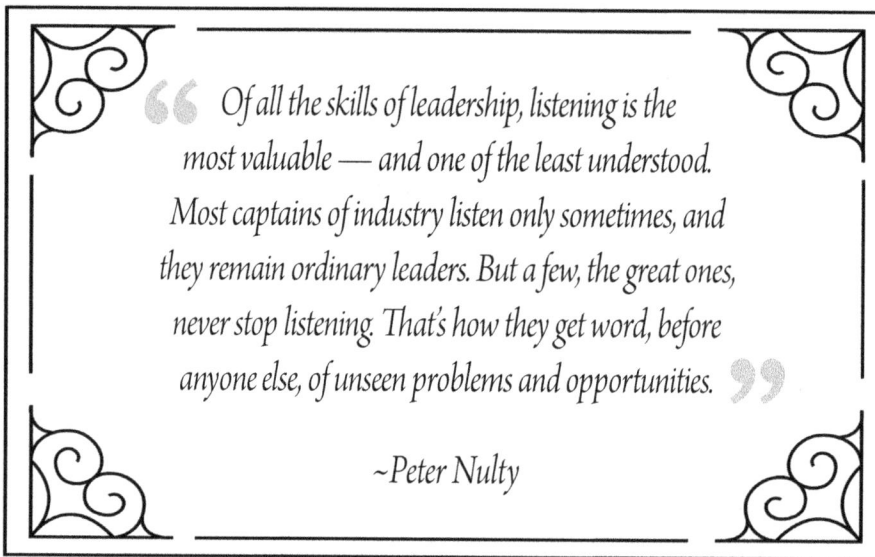

Great leaders who listen can be an early warning system.

Listening builds strong relationships with your team, but it does more than that. When you give your full attention, you start to notice the subtle things — early signs of problems, hidden opportunities, or unspoken concerns.

That insight gives you an edge as a leader.

This week, make it a point to truly listen to your team. Slow down, stay present, and ask questions that help you understand the meaning behind their words. What might you hear if you listened a little more closely?

Lead Your Team

I remind myself every morning:
Nothing I say this day will
teach me anything. So if I'm going
to learn, I must do it by listening.

~Larry King

Listening is one of the best ways to learn.

You never know where your next insight might come from — a new perspective, a casual comment, or even a question you hadn't thought to ask.

As a business leader, the more you listen, the more you understand the challenges and opportunities in front of you.

This week, practice listening with your full attention. Then pause and ask yourself: "What did I just learn?"

Sometimes, the greatest lessons come when we simply stay quiet and pay attention.

Lead Your Business

> *Emotional intelligence is the ability to recognize, understand, and manage our own emotions, and to recognize, understand, and influence the emotions of others.*
>
> ~Daniel Goleman

Emotional intelligence is a key part of strong leadership.

As leaders, our ability to recognize and manage our own emotions — and understand the emotions of others — often shapes how successful we are.

When we handle our emotions well, we respond more calmly, clearly and effectively in tough situations. And when we truly understand how our team is feeling, we build trust, connection, and influence.

This week, slow down and observe. How are you reacting to situations? What emotions do you notice in those around you?

Awareness is the first step to leading with emotional intelligence.

Lead Yourself

> *Emotional intelligence is the ability to sense,*
> *understand, and effectively apply the power*
> *and acumen of emotions as a source of human*
> *energy, information, connection, and influence.*
>
> ~Robert K. Cooper

Emotional intelligence is a powerful source of energy and connection.

I love the phrase "...apply the power and acumen of emotions as a source of human energy..." — it's a reminder that our emotions aren't just something to manage; they can fuel and inspire us.

Imagine what could happen if you tapped into that energy to uplift yourself and your team. This week, don't ignore emotions, learn from them and use them to lead with purpose and impact.

Lead Yourself

> *Great leaders move us. They ignite our passion and inspire the best in us. When we try to explain why they are so effective, we speak of strategy, vision, or powerful ideas. But the reality is much more primal: Great leadership works through the emotions.*
>
> ~ Daniel Goleman, Richard Boyatzis, & Annie McKee

Great leadership begins with emotion.

It's not just about vision or strategy — it's about connection. Emotions fuel motivation, build trust, and inspire action.

The most powerful leaders don't just manage tasks. They let their emotions be the spark that helps their team move forward with purpose.

This week, think about how you can tap into your own emotions — and those of your team — to spark energy, focus, and momentum.

Lead Your Team

> *As more and more artificial intelligence is entering into the world, more and more emotional intelligence must enter into leadership.*
>
> *~ Amit Ray*

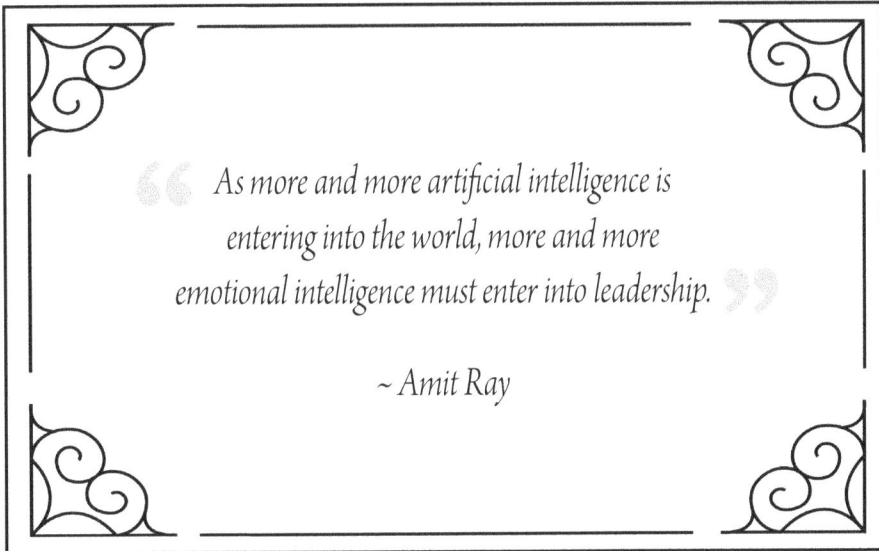

AI is powerful — but it's not a replacement for leadership.

Artificial Intelligence is an incredible tool. It can speed things up, automate tasks, and give us better data. But tools alone don't build strong businesses — people do. While AI might optimize performance, emotional intelligence inspires it.

As a business owner, your job is to lead both the tech and the team.

This week, pause and ask yourself, "Where can technology support my team? And where do people bring something tech can't — empathy, connection, creativity?"

Lead Your Business

FOCUS AND VISION

> 66 *You are more likely to acquire power by narrowing your focus and applying your energies, like the sun's rays, to a limited range of activities in a small number of domains.* 99
>
> ~ Jeffrey Pfeffer

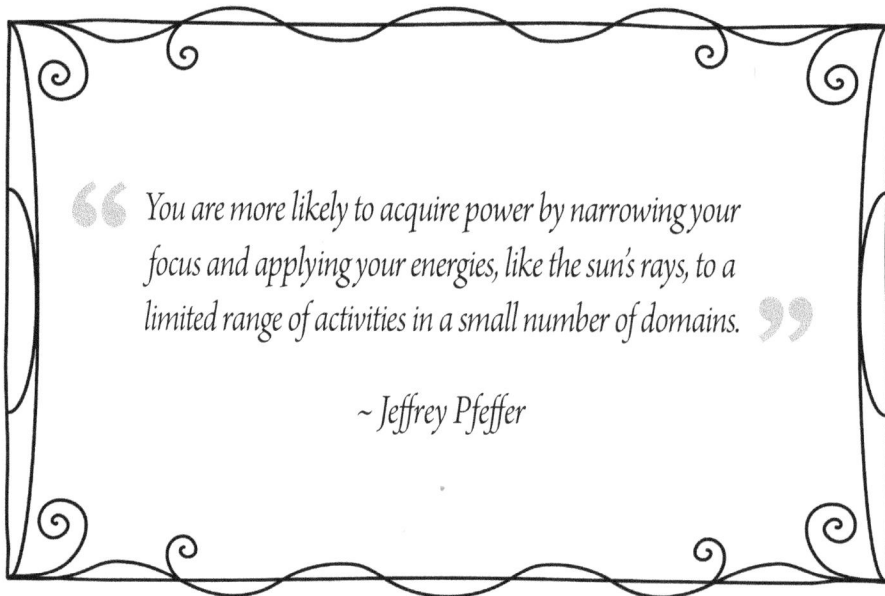

Focus is a quiet kind of power.

Strong leaders know it's not about doing more — it's about doing what matters most. I love the image of focusing your energy like the sun's rays: when your attention is concentrated, it becomes a powerful force.

This week, take a moment to reflect on how you're spending your time. Are you focused on the few key areas that truly move you forward?

Lead Yourself

What you stay focused on will grow.

~ Roy T. Bennett

What you focus on will grow.

As an entrepreneur, staying focused is one of your most powerful tools. But focus takes patience — results don't always show up right away.

Choose a few key areas in your business and give them your full energy and attention. Over time, you'll see progress.

And remember: focus works both ways. If you constantly dwell on problems, those will grow too. Where will you direct your focus this week?

Lead Your Business

> *The successful warrior is the average man, with laserlike focus.*
>
> *~Bruce Lee*

Success comes from laser-like focus.

A great leader, like a skilled warrior, doesn't try to do everything — they concentrate on what matters most.

This week, take a look at where your time and energy are going. Are you focused on just a few key priorities? What can you adjust to sharpen your focus even more?

Small shifts in attention can lead to big results.

Lead Yourself

> *Focus is a matter of deciding what things you're not going to do.*
>
> ~John Carmack

Focus isn't just about what you do — it's also about what you don't do.

Great leaders stay focused and help their teams do the same. That often means saying no to tasks, ideas, or distractions that don't align with the main goal.

This week, take a moment to reflect: What can you say "no" to, so your team can stay focused on what truly matters?

Lead Your Team

> *Focus on the solution, not the problem.*
>
> ~*Jim Rohn*

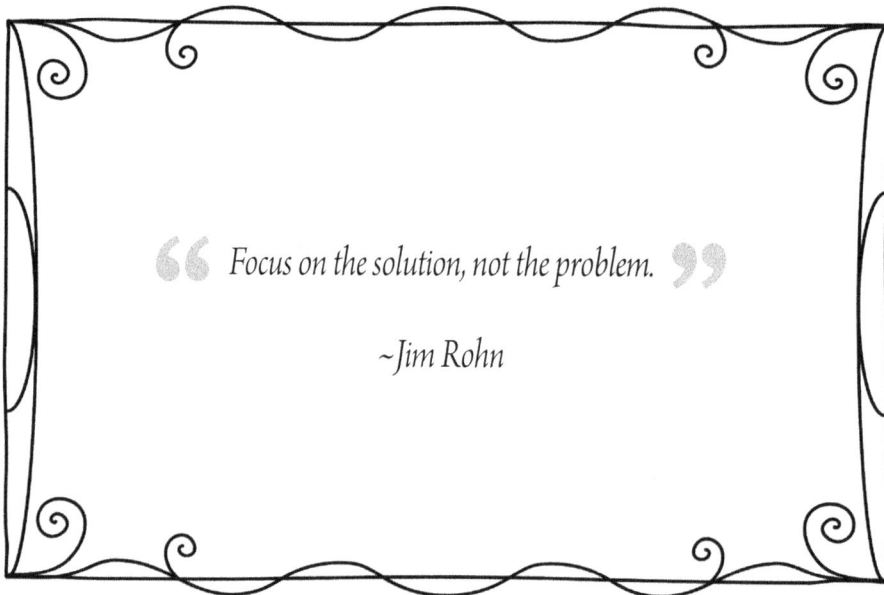

Don't get stuck on the problem — focus on the solution.

As entrepreneurs, it's easy to dwell on what's missing — not enough time, money, or support. But growth comes when you shift your focus from what's wrong to what can be done.

This week, take a fresh look at your current challenges. Brainstorm solutions, pick one or two, and put your energy into making them happen.

Progress starts when your focus shifts from the problem to the possibility.

Lead Your Business

> *Leadership is the capacity to translate a vision into reality.*
>
> ~*Warren Bennis*

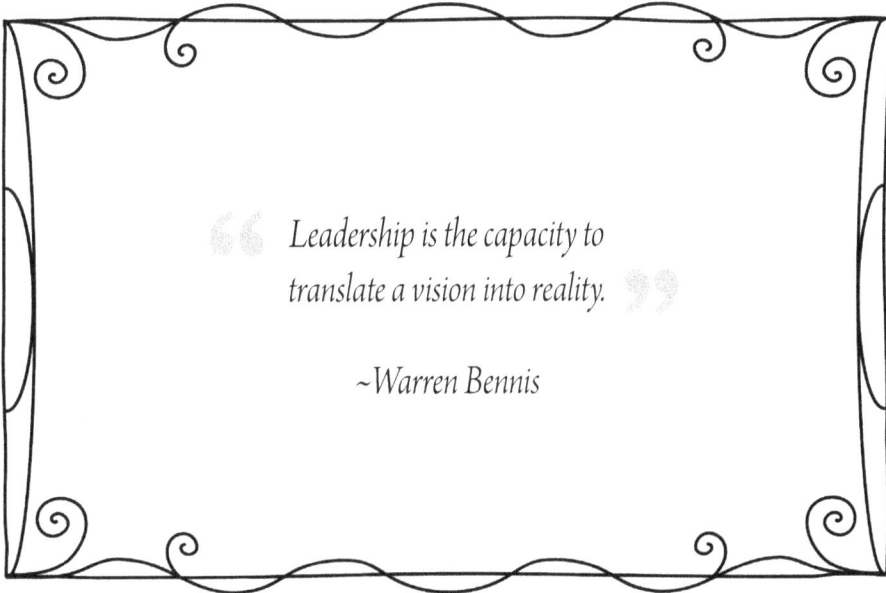

Leadership begins with a vision.

As the leader, it's your job to guide your business toward that vision and bring others along with you. The clearer your vision, the stronger your direction.

Take a moment this week to reflect: Is your vision clear and focused? Have you shared it in a way your team understands and feels inspired by?

Great leadership isn't about doing it all alone—it's about turning your vision into reality, together.

Lead Your Business

> *The greatest leaders mobilize others by coalescing people around a shared vision.*
>
> ~ Ken Blanchard

A clear vision means little if you keep it to yourself.

As a leader, your next step is to bring your team into that vision—so it's not just yours, but ours.

This week, ask yourself: "Have I shared my vision in a way that excites and motivates my team? What can I do to make them feel like they're part of it?"

Lead Your Team

> *A leader has the vision and conviction that a dream can be achieved. He inspires the power and energy to get it done.*
>
> ~ Ralph Lauren

A powerful vision is just the beginning.

As a leader, it's your job to bring that vision to life—and to energize your team with it. When people feel inspired, they don't just work harder—they work with purpose.

This week, think about this: How can you spark excitement about where your business is going? What can you say or do to help your team feel part of something bigger?

Inspiration turns ideas into action. Let your leadership set that energy in motion.

Lead Your Team

> 66 *Create a vision for the life you really want and*
> *then work relentlessly towards making it a reality.* 99
>
> ~ *Roy T. Bennett*

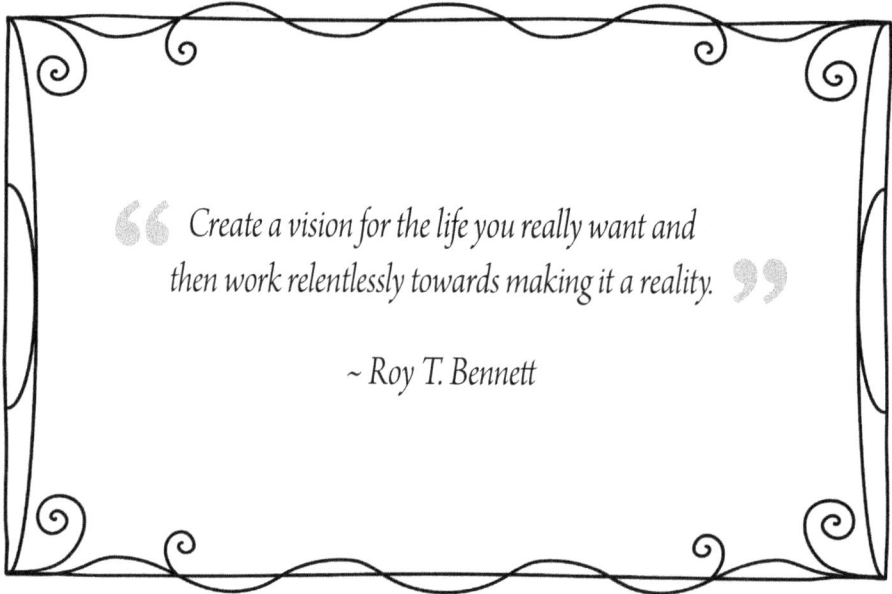

Your vision starts with you.

As an entrepreneur, it's important to know what kind of life you truly want—because your business should help you build that life, not take you away from it.

Once you're clear on your vision, let it guide your decisions, your habits, and your time.

This week, ask yourself: "What does my ideal life really look like? What small shift can I make to move closer to it?"

Lead your business by leading yourself first.

Lead Yourself

LEADERSHIP AND VALUES

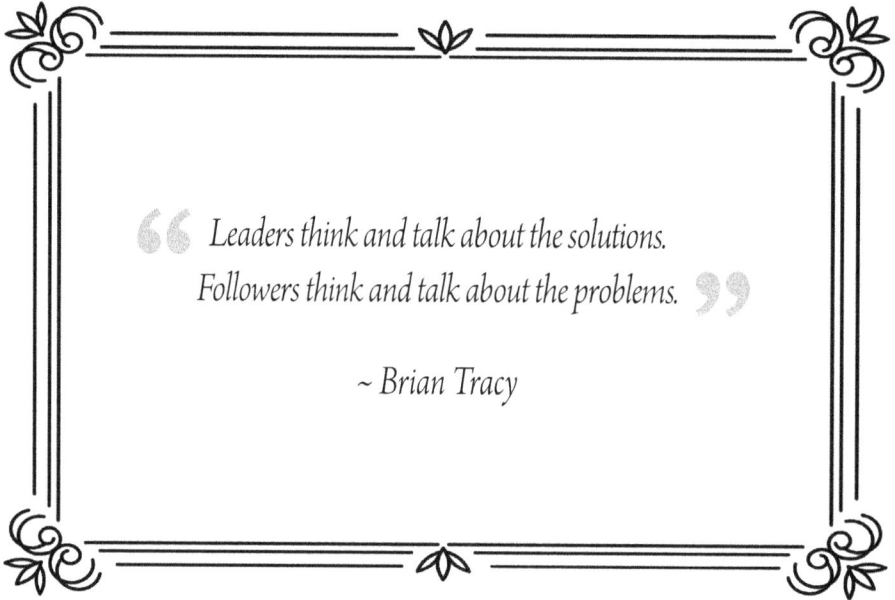

> *Leaders think and talk about the solutions.*
> *Followers think and talk about the problems.*
>
> ~ Brian Tracy

Are you solutions focused?

Are you focusing on solutions? Great leaders see opportunities and possibilities instead of getting stuck on challenges and problems.

This week, ask yourself "What solutions and opportunities can I highlight so my team feels energized to move forward?"

Lead Yourself

Think little goals and expect little achievements.
Think big goals and win big success.

~ David Joseph Schwartz

Are your goals big enough?

What are your plans for the coming year? Are your goals big enough? As the leader of your business, it's up to you to set the direction and vision.

Take time this week to review your goals. Will they lead you to the success you want? If not, adjust them to aim higher.

Lead Your Business

> " *How we think shows through in how we act. Attitudes are mirrors of the mind. They reflect thinking.* "
>
> ~David Joseph Schwartz

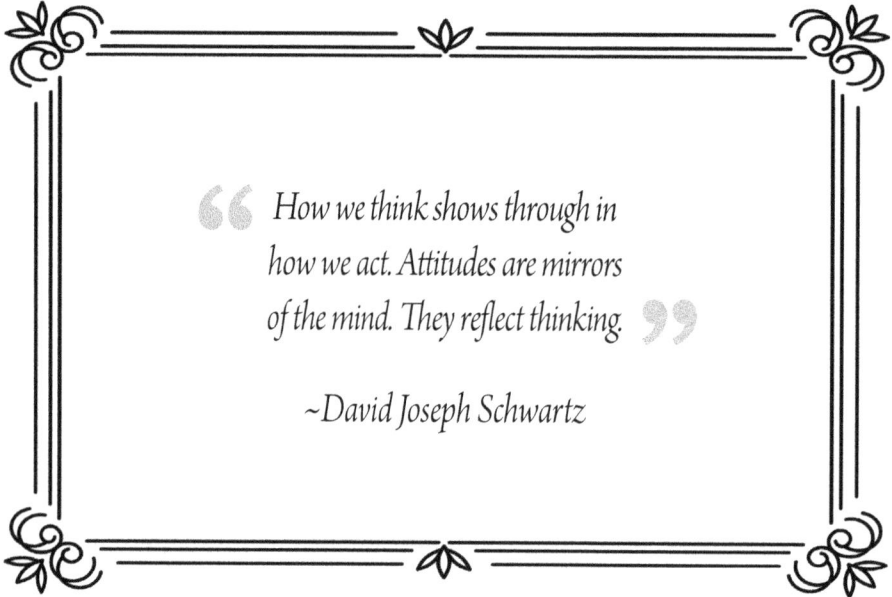

Your actions reveal your true intentions.

What truly matters to you—and are your actions aligned with it?

If not, take a moment to reflect: "If I really believe in this, what actions should I be taking?"

Lead Yourself

> *The growth and development of people
> is the highest calling of leadership.*
>
> ~Harvey S. Firestone

Identify the potential in your team members

Great leaders recognize the potential in their team members and help them grow into their best selves.

Investing in your team's development not only benefits them but also drives success for your business. Who are you actively supporting and nurturing into a leader?

Lead Your Team

> " *The best way to predict the future is to create it,*
> *and that starts with knowing what truly matters.* "
>
> *~Peter Drucker*

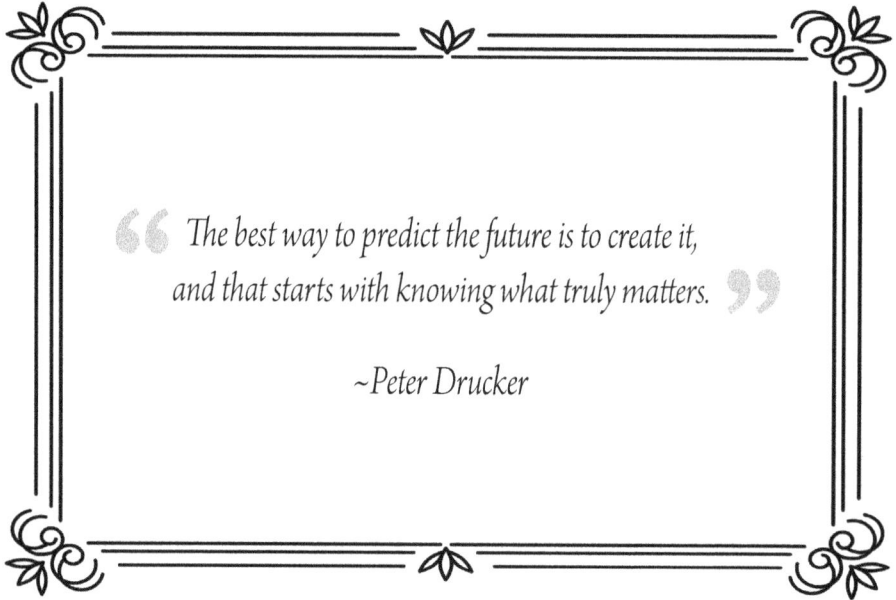

Let values guide decisions

Great leaders know that their values guide every decision they make. When planning for the future, they start by focusing on what truly matters— then take action to create the results they want.

This week, take a moment to reflect: How do your values shape the decisions you make in your business?

Lead Your Business

> *Leadership is about making the right decision, not the easy one.*
>
> ~*Unknown*

The right decision isn't always easy

Great leaders stay true to their values when making decisions. The right choice isn't always the easiest, but when it aligns with your values, you can trust it's the right one. As you make decisions this week, ask yourself: "Does this choice reflect my values?"

Lead Yourself

> *The key is not to prioritize what's on your schedule, but to schedule your priorities.*
>
> ~ Stephen R. Covey

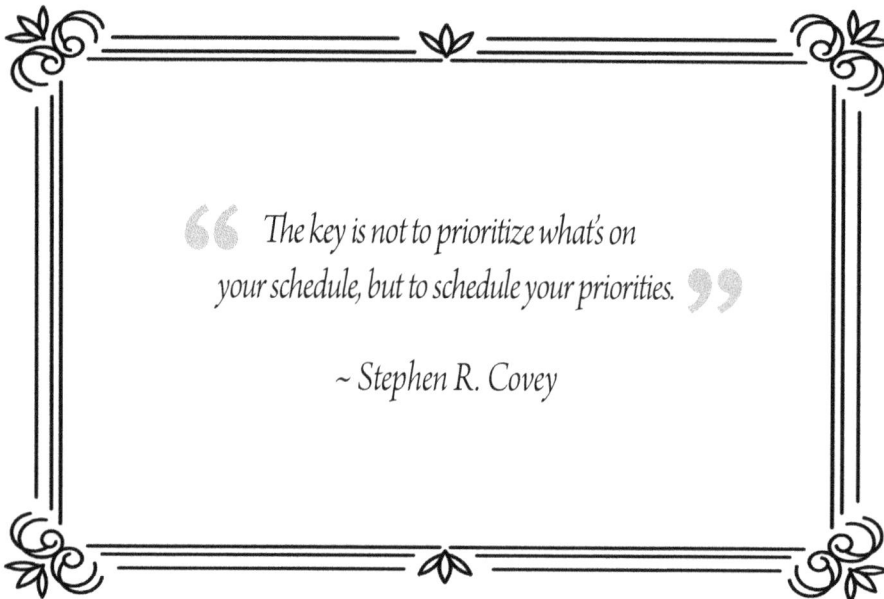

Does your schedule reflect your priorities?

A leader's schedule should reflect what truly matters. As you plan your week, take a moment to check—are you prioritizing tasks that align with your values? When your schedule reflects your values, you lead with purpose and clarity.

Lead Your Team

> *Values can't be just words on a page,*
> *to be effective they must shape action.*
>
> ~ Jeffrey Immelt

Great leaders turn their values into action.

How do your values shape the decisions you make? This week, take a moment to reflect—are your actions aligned with what you truly believe?

Lead Your Team

ABOUT THE AUTHOR

A leadership book that turns inspiration into intentional action

A certified professional coach, group facilitator and change-maker, Lynne Roe helps entrepreneurs, business leaders and non-profit leaders, develop a foundation of leadership that serves as a catalyst for growth. Applying knowledge and skills acquired over decades of working with small and large companies, and non-profits, she guides business owners and non-profit leaders in strategic planning, sound decision-making, leveraging the strengths of individual team members, and developing communications that build collaboration, respect, and trust. She provides clients with the tools to become outstanding leaders focused on transforming their organization for the future and serving as a positive force in their communities.

Lynne and her husband live in Northern New Jersey. Being an outdoor enthusiast, she loves to travel to beautiful locations and enjoy the scenery while biking, boating, skiing or hiking.